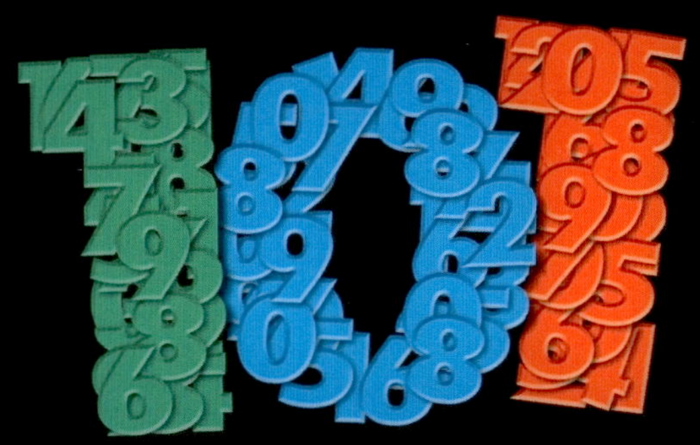

WAYS TO BEAT BOREDOM

Anna Claybourne

CONTENTS

BORED?

Did you know that you'll probably spend a third of your life asleep? And you'll spend over 2600 days in school. Wow! That's a lot of time. So your free time is *really* important. Don't waste it being bored!

How can you make the most of your time? Simple. All you need are some ideas – 101 to be exact! Now, 101 things might sound like a lot. But don't worry – you don't have to do everything. In fact, you don't even need to read this book from start to finish. You can start in the middle! Go on. Have a look and if you're feeling brave, take your first challenge.

I'm BORED.
What can I do?

1 Fun for Your Friends

We think there is an activity in here for everybody. Can you find one for each of your friends?

I've finished my computer game ...
Finished my book, too ...
Watch out for brain-boggling tricks, flying gumboots and funny moustaches! See ideas 10, 21 and 75.

2 PUT ON A PLAY

Would you like to be an actor one day? Why not start now? Get your friends together and put on a play. Parents, friends and pets can be the audience!

A play is really quite simple. All you need is:

- a story
- dialogue (what people say)
- actions (what people do).

How about retelling a story you know? Choose your favourite book or film and turn it into a play.

The Creepy Creek Mystery

Scene 1

Mr Snark: Welcome to Creepy Creek, my dear!

Emily: Thank you. My sister Gertie should be here any minute ...

[a knock at the door]

Mr Snark: Who's that?

Emily: Gertie?

Top Tip!
Start a new line each time a different character speaks.

3 Set the Stage

Use cardboard, paper or even an old sheet to make a painted **backdrop**.

4 Dress Up

Make costumes for your characters using old clothes or scrap material.

5 Make a Poster

Include a big picture and the names of all the stars!

6 Make It Real

Make a play about something that really happened to you.

7 New Adventures

Think of your favourite TV characters. Can you make a play about them?

8 Big Number

Add a song and dance routine to your play.

9 Curtain Call

For the finishing touch, use a sheet to make a stage curtain.

If you have a spy in your play, why not try ideas 71 to 76?

10 AMAZE YOUR FRIENDS!

Tell your friends you can step through a postcard. They don't believe you? Then do it before their very eyes!

WISH YOU WERE HERE!

1. Take a normal, boring postcard that no one wants.

2. Fold the card in half lengthways.

3. Then cut lines in the card as in this diagram.

A

B

4. Carefully cut along the fold from point A to point B.

Top Tip!
Practise on your own first so you get it right!

5. Carefully open up the card into a big loop and step through it. Ta-daaa!

11

Curious Coin

Take a large coin. Fix the coin between the teeth of two forks. Balance the coin on the edge of a glass. Magic!

12

Biscuit Business

Challenge your friends to eat three dry biscuits in three minutes. No water allowed!

13

Paper-fold Puzzle

How many times can you keep folding a piece of paper in half?

14

Mysterious Mobius Strip

Take a strip of paper. Twist one end over, then stick the two ends together to make a loop. Cut down the length of the strip. What happens?

15

Floating Hands

Stand in a doorway and press the backs of your hands hard against the frame for one minute. When you step out, your hands will have a mind of their own!

16

Balancing Act

Stand on one foot, then close your eyes. Count to 10. Do you start to fall over?

17

What a Hoot!

Cup your hands together. Leave a gap between your thumbs. Blow across it at the right angle to make an owl sound.

18 MAKE A BOOMERANG

Ever wanted to throw a boomerang? Now you can, without hurting yourself or anyone else!

You will need:

- cardboard
- scissors
- pens and pencils

1. Trace the boomerang shape shown here onto cardboard. Then cut it out.
2. Fold down the edges, shown by the dotted lines on the outline.
3. Decorate your boomerang.
4. Throw your boomerang.

Top Tip!

- Hold your boomerang with the thin edge at the front.
- Swing your arm in a curving motion to throw it.

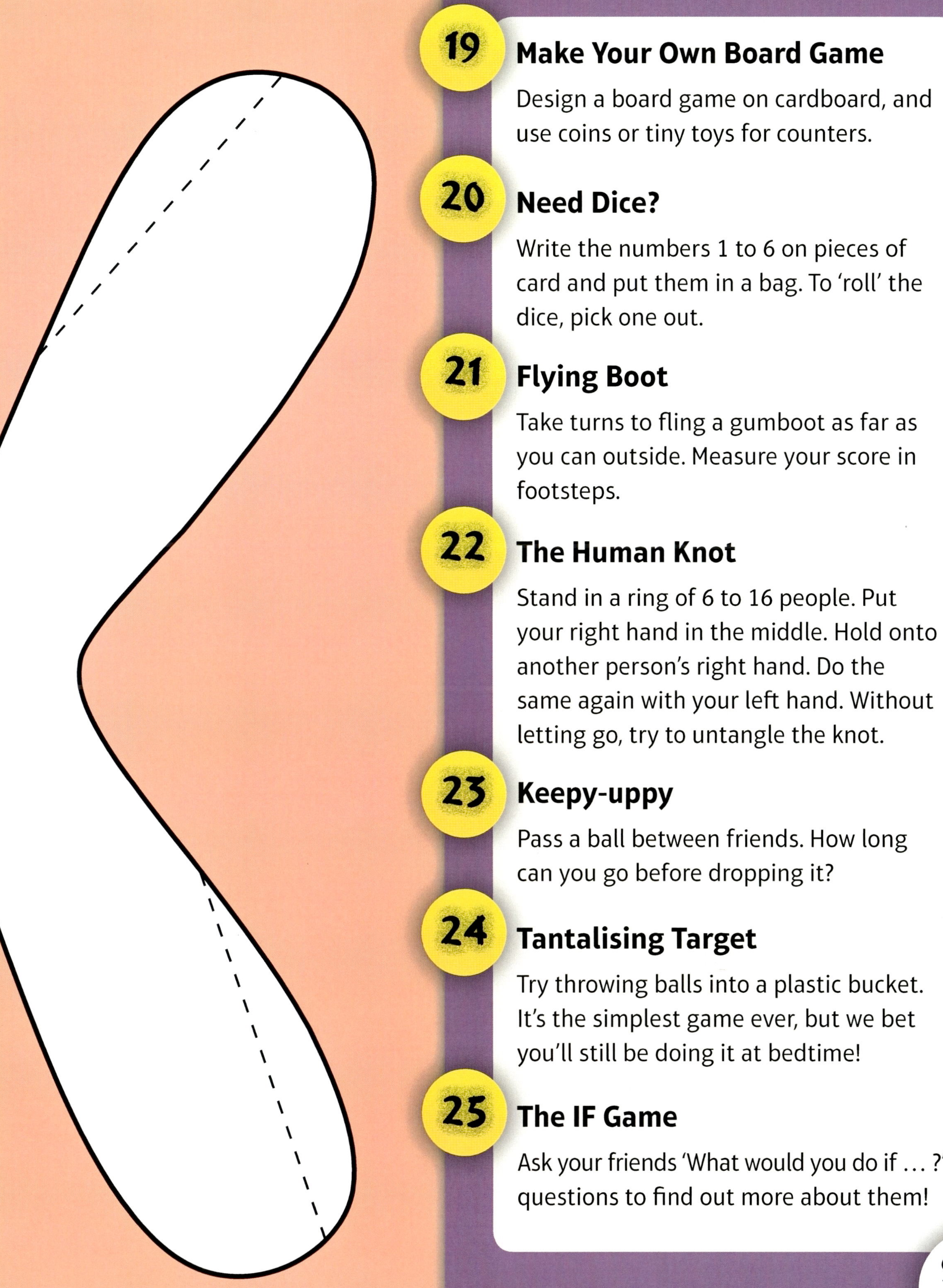

19 Make Your Own Board Game

Design a board game on cardboard, and use coins or tiny toys for counters.

20 Need Dice?

Write the numbers 1 to 6 on pieces of card and put them in a bag. To 'roll' the dice, pick one out.

21 Flying Boot

Take turns to fling a gumboot as far as you can outside. Measure your score in footsteps.

22 The Human Knot

Stand in a ring of 6 to 16 people. Put your right hand in the middle. Hold onto another person's right hand. Do the same again with your left hand. Without letting go, try to untangle the knot.

23 Keepy-uppy

Pass a ball between friends. How long can you go before dropping it?

24 Tantalising Target

Try throwing balls into a plastic bucket. It's the simplest game ever, but we bet you'll still be doing it at bedtime!

25 The IF Game

Ask your friends 'What would you do if … ?' questions to find out more about them!

26 MAKE A PAPER BOAT

When can paper float? When it's your very own paper boat!

1. Fold a large piece of rectangular paper in half.

2. Open up your paper and fold it in half the other way.

3. Fold the top corners over to the middle line.

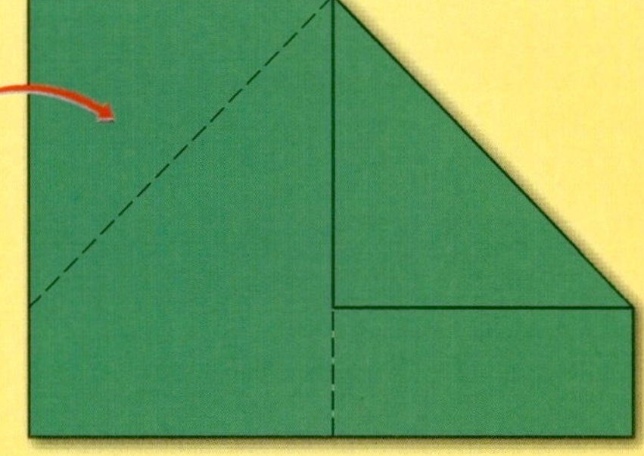

4. Fold up the two bottom flaps, one to each side.

5. Grab the bottom flaps here and pull towards you.

6. Press flat into a diamond.

7. Fold up each bottom half to make a triangle.

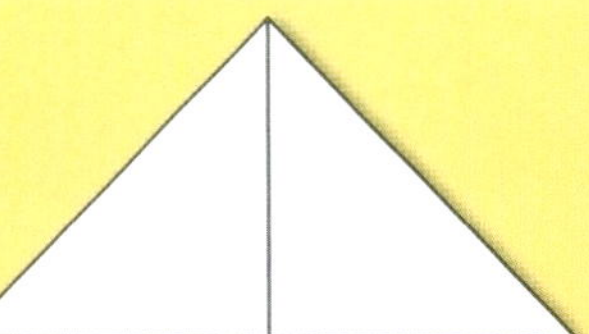

8. Grab the bottom of your triangle and pull towards you. Press flat into a diamond.

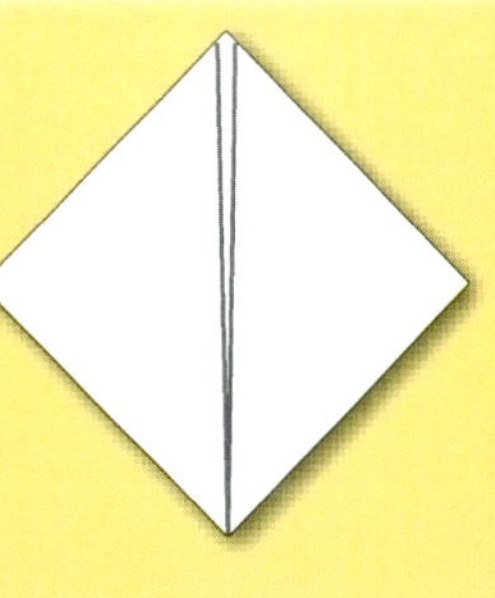

9. Grab the top corners and pull out to the sides. There's your boat!

Your finished boat is ready to set sail.

27 The Great Boat Race

Blow your paper boats along a tray of water using straws. Who can reach the other side first?

28 Water Music

Collect some glass bottles that are all the same size. Fill them up with different levels of water. Get a spoon and tap out a tune!

29 Daredevil Diver

Hold a ruler on the edge of a bath. Stand a toy figure on the end outside the bath. Press down on the other end of the ruler. *Boinngg!* Your diver will leap into the water.

30 Blowing Bubbles

Make your own bubble potion. Mix together 7 parts water, 3 parts dishwashing liquid and 1 part glycerine. Now use an old wire coat-hanger, dip it in the potion and bubble away!

31 Marbly Milk

Fill a jar lid with milk. Add a few drops of different coloured food dye. Dip a cotton bud in dishwashing liquid and swirl it in the milk. Watch what happens!

32 Bombs Away!

Grab your friends and make two teams. Using water balloons, try to get each other as wet as possible! Make sure you are outside!

33 NATURE HUNT

How well do you know the area you live in? Take the Nature Hunt challenge and see what you can discover.

You can do this in your backyard or a local park. Copy the table and see how much you can find.

Can you spot …	Draw/write what you see
six different-shaped leaves	gum leaf
five different seeds	
four different kinds of birds	magpie honey-eater
three different flowers	
two creepy-crawlies (insects, spiders, slugs or snails)	
one animal's home	bird's nest

Top Tip! You could make it into a competition and have a prize for the winner.

34 Make Your Own

You don't need to stick to our nature hunt. Write your own to suit the season and the place you live in.

35 Catch a Spider's Web

Tie three twigs together in a triangle. Stand it outside. After a few days, check to see if a spider has set up home! But just look – don't touch!

36 Make It Grow

Collect seeds from fruit. Plant them in a pot and see if they grow. Remember to water them!

37 The Longest Daisy Chain Ever!

Pick a daisy and use your thumbnail to make a hole in the stalk. Slip another daisy through, and keep going!

38 Spot It

Make sketches in a notebook of the things you spot on your nature walk. Note where and when you saw them.

39 Skimming Stones On Water

Hold a flat stone with your **index finger** against one edge. Flick the stone as you throw. It should bounce over the water!

HAVE A PIZZA PARTY

**Be good to your friends – throw a party!
Be good to your mum and dad
– help do the cooking!**

How to Make the Perfect Pizza

You will need:

3 cups of flour
½ tsp salt
1 tsp sugar
1 tsp dried yeast
1 cup warm water
1 tbsp olive oil
Tomato sauce
Grated cheese
Your favourite toppings

What to do:

- Put the dry ingredients in a bowl.
- Add the water and olive oil.
- Mix it into a ball.
- **Knead** the dough, then leave it for 1 hour.
- Roll out the dough into a pizza shape.
- Add tomato sauce, grated cheese and your favourite toppings.
- Get a grown-up to cook it for 20 minutes.

For party game ideas, see ideas 10 to 17 and 22.

Top Tip!
It's important to get the measurements right. Here's what they mean:
tsp – teaspoon
tbsp – tablespoon

41 Dress Fancy

Give your party an Italian theme. Have your guests dress up as Italian opera singers, soccer players or gondoliers.

42 Get Creative

Design and send invitations to your friends. Don't forget the place, date, time and theme.

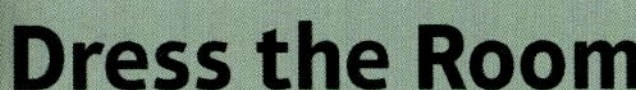

43 Dress the Room

Make decorations to match your theme.

44 Game On

Make sure you prepare a few party games.

45 Party Punch

Make **punch**. Mix equal parts tropical fruit juice, lemonade and fizzy water in a bowl. Add fruit.

46 Tune Up

Put together songs or music to play.

47 Yummy Bugs!

Make half a pack of jelly. When set, put creepy-crawly lollies on the jelly. Then make the rest of the jelly and pour on top.

GO STARGAZING

The next time it's a dark, clear night – look up! In the sky you should see lots of beautiful stars. These stars make up shapes called **constellations**. Why not try to spot these two?

The Saucepan

Southern Cross

The Southern Cross constellation can be seen nearly all year round almost anywhere in Australia. It has five bright stars.

49 **Look Up**

On a dark, clear night, away from any lights, you might see the Milky Way. It's made up of billions of stars!

50 **Make a Wish**

If you see a streak of light zoom across the sky, it's a shooting star. Don't forget to make a wish!

51 **Moon Diary**

Sketch how the Moon looks each night. How does it change?

52 **Shadow Shapes**

Shine a torch at the wall in a dark room. Put your hands in front of it and see what animal shapes you can make.

53 **Moth-spotting**

In a garden, spread out a white sheet and shine a torch onto it. Moths will come to it and you can get a close look at them.

54 **Spooky Stories**

On a dark night, tell each other your favourite spooky tales. Don't have nightmares!

55 **Scary Face**

Shine a torch up at your face from under your chin. How scary can you look?

56 MOVING MONSTER

How do you catch a moving monster? By drawing it in a flip book. Flick the pages and watch it come to life.

You will need:

- a small notepad with lots of pages
- a pencil or crayons

1. Draw a circle at the edge of the page.

2. Turn the page. Now draw the same circle but move it slightly. Repeat this two more times.

3. Turn the page. Now make your circle into a monster.

4. Turn the page. Draw the same monster with its arms up in the air.

Top Tip!
In order to make your monster move for longer, only make a small change each time.

5. Turn the page. Draw the monster with its arms back down.

6. Test it! Flick the pages and watch the monster move. Could you make your flip book better by making the changes on each page even smaller?

57 Flip More

Try making another flip book. Can you make a baby monster hatch from an egg?

58 Never-ending Story

Write four words of a story – "Once upon a time". Then pass it to a friend to write four more words. Keep passing on the story … it may never end!

59 Write to a Writer

Write a letter or email to your favourite author. (Be polite!) You might even get a reply back.

60 Start a Diary

Try to write down something funny, interesting or sad that happens to you each day.

61 Be a Journalist

Start your own magazine. It could be about anything!

62 Swap It

Swap books with your friends. You might discover some great stories.

63 ART SPLAT!

If you like to make a mess, this is for you! Try being a modern artist and make this picture.

You will need:

- empty yoghurt containers
- runny paint
- string

Get painting

1. Spread out *lots* of newspaper.
2. Place a big piece of plain paper on top of the newspaper.
3. Ask a grown-up to make a small hole in the bottom of each yoghurt container.
4. Tie string around each container. Leave 30 cm of string free.
5. Half-fill each yoghurt container with a different colour paint.
6. Now lift the containers by their strings and swing them over the paper.

You could even make your art into invitations for idea 42.

Top Tip!
Make sure you use lots of old newspaper and wear old clothes. This is really messy!

This style of painting is known as abstract art.

64 No Paintbrushes

Try painting with different things such as sticks, tissue paper or even your toes!

65 Take a Line for a Walk

Draw a picture without taking your pencil off the paper.

66 Doodle Bug

Doodle over a piece of paper. Then fill in the shapes with different colours.

67 Art Without Eyes

Put on a blindfold. Can you draw a house, a person, a flower or a rocket?

68 No Hands

Try drawing a picture by holding a pen between your toes.

69 What Next?

Once your works of art are dry, make them into cards.

70 Steal Their Style

Find an artist you really like and try to copy their style.

71 SPY WRITING

Ever wondered how spies send secret messages? You can do it yourself – with invisible ink!

For your ink, use lemon juice. Write your message on a piece of paper using a small paintbrush. Wait for it to dry. Then it's ready to send.

To see the message, your fellow spies must leave it on a warm heater, or in bright sunlight. The letters will turn brown and become readable.

Come to my spy party.
Details to follow.

Top Tip!
You can use apple juice or clear vinegar instead.

72 Keep It Secret

Write down the alphabet and give each letter a different number. This is your code. Write your message in the code. Only someone with a copy of the code will be able to crack it.

73 Pass the Word

All good spy clubs need a password. It should be a made-up word that no one will guess, such as 'squirdlepip'.

74 Wrap It Up

Wrap a strip of paper around a pen in a spiral. Write your message along it, then unwrap it. Your spy contacts can only read it by wrapping it around the same-sized pen.

75 Guess Who?

Spies often need a disguise. Wear dark glasses, a hat and even a fake moustache.

76 Speak Gibberish

Drive your parents bonkers by speaking in code. Simply add a short code word to the middle of every syllable you say. Try cracking this code: Mu**og**m's pr**og**ese**og**nt i**og**s i**og**n m**og**y ro**og**om.

77 BRRR-ILLIANT ICE SCULPTURE

When the weather's freezing cold, make an ice sculpture.

You will need:

- modelling clay
- leaves, stones, sticks
- ribbon or string
- water

1. Make a hollow mould out of modelling clay.
2. Then put leaves, stones and sticks in it.
3. Carefully fill the mould with water.
4. Place a loop of ribbon in the top and leave it to freeze in the freezer.
5. When it's solid, take off the modelling clay.
6. Hang up your sculpture outside in the cold, winter weather.

Top Tip!
For a more colourful sculpture, add a drop of food dye to your water.

78 Christmas in July

Christmas is too much fun to have just once a year! Bake some gingerbread men, hang up some tinsel and have a cold-weather "Christmas in July" party with your friends.

79 Grow Some Ice Spikes

Pour some distilled water (which you can buy from your local supermarket) into an ice-cube tray and freeze overnight. The next morning, you should find some ice "**stalagmites**" have formed.

80 Go Team!

Watch your local footy team play a home game. Form a cheering section with your friends or family. Remember to wear your team's colours!

81 In the Swim

Just because it's cold outside doesn't mean you can't get wet! Head indoors for a spot of swimming in a heated pool.

82 Winter Warmer

Chase away the winter chills with a warm drink. Mix three teaspoons of hot chocolate powder into a cup of warm milk. Top with cream, mini marshmallows or chocolate flakes. Yum!

Too warm for ice sculptures?
Try idea 91 instead.

83 CORNFLOUR SLIME

Investigate the weird world of slime! This isn't any ordinary slime though! Make it and find out why.

You will need:

- 2 cups of **cornflour**
- a bowl
- water
- green food colouring

84 Slime Ball

Add more cornflour to your mix to make a slime ball. What happens when you drop it on the table?

What to Do

Put the cornflour in a bowl. Add water bit by bit until it's a gluggy mix. Add a few drops of green food colouring to make it look like slime.

Now for the fun stuff! See what happens to the slime when you:

- stir the slime slowly
- stir the slime quickly
- hit the slime.

85 Does Other Slime Do This?

What happens if you make slime using normal flour? Can you do the same tricks?

86 Defy Gravity

Completely fill a paper cup with water. Lie a postcard on top. Turn them upside down. Now take your hand away. The postcard will stay!

87 Which Is Which?

How can you tell a boiled egg from a raw egg? Spin each egg then stop them. When you let go, the raw egg will start spinning again!

88 Taste Test

Try tasting slivers of apple, raw onion and raw cabbage while holding your nose. Can you tell which is which?

89 Test Your Reaction Time

Ask a friend to hold a ruler in the air. Hold your thumb and finger apart at the bottom of the ruler. Get your friend to drop the ruler. Measure where you caught the ruler.

90 Confuse Your Brain

Try moving your right foot **clockwise** while drawing the number six in the air with your right hand.

Top Tip!
Do the really messy activities outside.

91 SAND ANIMALS

A day at the beach is great fun. But once you've had a swim and eaten your lunch, what can you do? Well, how about making sand animals?

Make a pile of sand and shape it into an animal. Try a dolphin, whale, snake, turtle or a curled-up cat.

Top Tip!
Use sand that's a bit wet for the best sand sculptures.

Sand sculptures can be simple like this turtle or elaborate like this fairytale scene.

92 World's Biggest!

The biggest sandcastle ever made was over 9 metres tall! Yours probably won't be that big but make the biggest, most beautiful castle you can.

93 X Marks the Spot

Make a map of an imaginary island in the sand. You could even bury some treasure!

94 Monster Feet

Use sand to give someone enormous feet, with huge warty toes. (Shells make good warts.)

95 27, 28, 29 ...

Seagulls are a part of going to the beach. How many can you count in a day?

96 Fly a Kite

Two sticks, a plastic bag, sticky tape and string can make a perfect kite.

97 Rock Pools

What creatures are lurking in the rock pools? Look closely under stones and among the seaweed.

98 Beach Cricket

Grab a bat and a tennis ball, make new friends on the beach and play beach cricket. Howzat!

99 Shrink Your Friends

Put a beach ball on the ground. Get a friend to stand about 30 steps away. Move your head so that their feet line up with the top of the ball. Take a photo. They will look tiny!

100 Thong Throwing

A summer version of gumboot throwing.
See idea 21.

101 RELAX!

Phew! You must be worn out. It's great to have loads to do, but don't forget to take some time to rest.

Enjoy your free time. Before you know it, it will be time to go back to school – or time for bed! Sleep well.

GLOSSARY

backdrop painted scenery at the back of a stage

clockwise in the direction the hands of a clock move

constellations patterns that seem to appear in the stars

cornflour fine flour made from corn (also called maize)

index finger finger you use for pointing

knead mix by pressing, folding and pulling

punch party drink made by mixing lots of drinks together

stalagmites columns of rock rising from the floor of caves

INDEX